Mixed Emotions

– RENETHA FENTON –

An environmentally friendly book printed and bound in England by
www.printondemand-worldwide.com

Mixed Sources
Product group from well-managed
forests, and other controlled sources
www.fsc.org Cert no. TT-COC-002641
© 1996 Forest Stewardship Council

FSC

PEFC
PEFC/16-33-415

PEFC Certified
This product is
from sustainably
managed forests
and controlled
sources
www.pefc.org

This book is made entirely of chain-of-custody materials

http://www.fast-print.net/bookshop

MIXED EMOTIONS
Copyright © Renetha Fenton 2015

A catalogue record for this book is available from the British Library

ISBN 978-178456-224-3

First published 2015 by
FASTPRINT PUBLISHING
Peterborough, England.

I thank God for the inspiration and ability to write this book and, to my son Gert for his contribution to some of the poems. I would also like to thank Anjulette, Susan and Miye for their help and, to my publisher for all the work they have done to make it a success.

The Match Maker

He was tall, handsome and physically fit.
His attitude and body language made me sick.
Rich and powerful was his father.
He being wealthy captured the heart of my mother.
She decided to be a matchmaker
And encouraged us to be together.

Mother wanted me to marry Calvin
But I was not in love with him.
For my heart belonged to Alvin.
Spring, summer, autumn or winter
Mother found an occasion to invite him over for dinner.

Dinner at our house became a regular thing with Calvin.
Reluctantly, I ended the relationship with Alvin.
It felt like I had committed a sin.
I wanted my mother to be proud of me,
I did what I knew would make her happy.

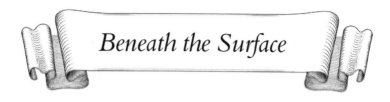

Beneath the Surface

On the night of our engagement party,
I saw my fiancée flirting with Mary.
I realised then that he was a womaniser.
I could not dare tell my mother.
She thought she had found me the perfect man
And she wanted him to be my husband.
A few months after I became his wife
Abuse played a major part in my life.
At nights when I went to bed
All the nasty words would echo in my head.
Sometimes, I thought I would be better off dead.

Whenever I had a black eye or any other,
I would avoid going to see my mother.
For all the horrible things she had seen,
I did not want her to feel any worse than she has been.
If I had stayed with Alvin
I probably would not have been in the situation I was in.

However eighteen months later
My marriage was finally over.
I am my mother's only daughter
And I did a lot of things to please her.
But when I was in that difficult situation,
I wished I had made my own decision.
Thank God I survived that episode of my life
And was free to become Alvin's wife.

Together Again

Reluctantly, I had to let her go to another,
I did not want her to disrespect or disobey her mother.
My father did not want me to marry her either,
But it was a risk I was willing to take
Even though he thought it would be a mistake.
My desire for her was tempting me,
I did not want her to commit adultery
So I moved to another part of the country
And there I waited patiently.
Two years after her marriage was over
We eventually found each other.
I thanked God for sparing her life
For now she has become my beautiful wife.

The Interview

On a cold and windy day in February
I had an interview at two-thirty.
When the phone rang
I thought something had gone wrong.
I quickly picked up the receiver,
On the other end was my sister-in-law.

She had called to remind me
About her birthday party.
I was relieved to hear her voice and took a seat,
As my heart returned to its regular beat.
I thanked her for reminding me.
I had completely forgotten about her party.

All I had thought about was the interview.
I wanted that job desperately.
The days and hours suited me perfectly.
The job I had was only temporary.
I wanted something permanently.

Day after day I waited patiently
For a reply from that specific company.
A few weeks later I received the letter
And I finally got the job I was hoping for.

Farewell

My dear friends and colleagues,
The time has come for me to leave.
I am not resigning from the company
I will be at another branch within the country.

I have no intentions of leaving this job.
It is the best one I've ever had.
The branch up north is much bigger
I will probably have to work a bit harder.

Do not worry much about me
I will continue to enjoy my work with the company.
I will do my very best,
To make sure it is a success.

I am going to miss you all terribly.
But I will visit, occasionally.
Whoever replaces me
I hope they will do their job properly.

It has been a pleasure working with you.
Moving up north is something I have to do.
Do not abuse your power.
Work as a team and communicate with each other.
It will help to ease the pressure.

Ninety-One Steps

When I was transferred over here in two thousand and five,
The situation took a different toll on my life.
I had a physical condition which didn't seem to matter.
The ninety-one steps I had to climb daily did not make it any
    easier.

The fifty-nine steps to the locker room would probably keep me
    fit,
I need not worry about purchasing an exercise kit.
The thirty-two steps from the locker room to the sales floor,
Made it more difficult for me to endure.

At busy times when I want to have a wee
I had to notify a supervisor immediately.
Otherwise, I would probably wet my panty
Going back up those steps to the toilet
Where I would actually have a wee.

I never intended to leave that job.
It was the best one I ever had.
Due to my physical condition
I had to make a very difficult decision.

At my age, I definitely had to face the fact.
Standing for hours behind a till puts too much pressure on my
    back.
Reluctantly I made a decision about my job.
The alternative was to terminate my contract.

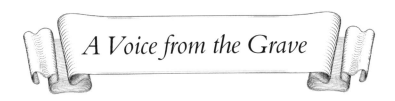

A Voice from the Grave

My wonderful children, family, relatives, work colleagues and
   friends,
My life has suddenly come to an end.
My loving mother and Ted,
Do not wait any more for me before going to bed.
I know that this is not what you expected it to be.
At the age of thirty-two, I did not expect to die so early.
I had many close accident calls,
But this one had outdone them all.
I did not see the lorry in front of me.
Probably, it was not to be.
The impact from the collision killed me instantly.
Then the van exploded and burned me beyond recognition,
And left my body in a horrible condition.
Mum, I know you would like to take one last look at me
But, I am not a very pleasant sight to see.
However, I know it would not cloud any memories you have of
   me.
Try not to worry much about me, God knows best.
He knew I would not want to be cooped up in a hospital bed.
Now that my work here on earth is done
I must go back to where I belong.
You all are sorry that I am not around physically,
But take a good look around and you will see,
I am right beside you spiritually.

My Son

You were a kind, loving and respectable son, brother and dad.
You have never done anything to make me sad.
I looked for your boots in the corridor,
I listened for the sound of your snoring, as I passed by your
     bedroom door.
Your number is still in my phone.
I wished that one day, you could come back home.
You gave me two beautiful grandchildren
And with their mother's permission,
I will help to guide them in the right direction.
Son, I did want to take one last look at you.
The family thought that it was not a good thing to do.
They could not give me a full description of what was left of you
So, I did what I had to do.
I called the officer who was in charge of the investigation
And I was satisfied with her description.
Your face was not like the handsome son I once knew,
Your missing toes were the perfect clue.
I knew then, it was you.
Now I accepted the fact that you are dead,
I will no longer wait to see you, before going to bed.
Surprisingly, you came into my life.
Unexpectedly, you went out like a light.
Although that we are apart
You will always be in my heart.
Our God and heavenly Father above
Know the depth of our precious love.
His love for you was greater than mine.
He took you, and left me behind.

I know that your work here is done,
And your new life has just begun.
But, you are and forever will be, my son.

The Abuse

I loved him with all my heart.
I promised nothing would ever keep us apart.
Then, my pregnancy took him by surprise,
And I did not like the look I saw in his eyes.
That night when I went to bed
I wondered what was going through his head.

Towards the end of my first trimester,
My sweet relationship had turned, not sour, but bitter.
As my tummy began to expand
I would often feel the weight of his hands.
Minutes later he would apologize and I would forgive him.
I believe that for him, becoming a father had not sunk in.

At the end of my second trimester
The abuse was worse than ever.
Sometimes, I could barely get out of bed.
I thought that one day, we may end up dead.
Looking forward to the birth gave me the strength to survive.
I could not afford to let him ruin our lives.

I decided not to take his abuse anymore.
I left him a note and walked out the door.
Despite the fact he had mistreated me,
The baby was born as healthy as could be.
And I thanked God for his love and mercy towards me.

The Message

This message comes direct from my heart,
I will love you till death do us part.
Every morning I hope and pray,
You will love me in the same special way.

Over my dead body I will let you get hurt,
Verily I say, you are more to life than it is worth.
Our secret, it can never be free.
We never had the chance for it to be.

Illegal Love

There are a few women in my life
Why did I fall for you?
Is it the situation or the time?
It does not matter because it is still a crime.
I am not supposed to love you the way I do.
Our friendship, I have threatened, the barrier I have reached.
The lights in my head flash breech! Breech!
Am I man enough to stand the consequences I would face?
Would I withstand the remarks or would I do an about-turn and
    walk?
Yet, just a few things I think of everyday
As I force myself to keep this illegal love at bay.

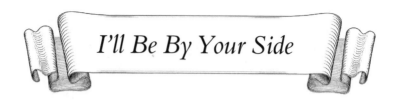

I'll Be By Your Side

When life seems rough and times get hard
And you start to think that there is no God,
Just know that the reason you are still here
It is because of God and the people who care.
I will do my best to make you smile.
I hope to be in your life for a very long time.
Whatever disappointments the universe sends
I will be right there by your side, my best friend.

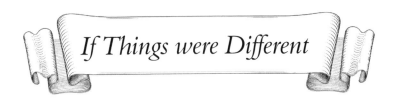

If Things were Different

If things were different and love was not blind
I would keep you safe for a lifetime.
If I had noticed earlier that you were the one
Our happiness together would have outshone the sun.
How much I love you and the years I have known you,
For sure, you would have been mine.
And we would be together for a lifetime.
I almost drove myself mad from all the thinking.
The wishing, praying and dreaming
So many feelings and thoughts; all, I had to keep at bay.
I was too afraid of losing you even for a day.
I may never find out how much you love me,
Because I preferred our friendship to be as perfect as it could be.
As your earth angel, I will always be in your life
Although you may never be mine or even become my wife.

Dear Mother

Through the rough and tough, your love we have always had
And you made us laugh whenever we were sad.
Whatever situation life throws our way
You always find something positive to say
That helps us to look at life in a different way.
We know we are special; you treat us all the same.
You told us to be there for each other because life is not a game.
You have more children but only three of us remain
And we know your love for us remains the same.
You are the main woman in our life from beginning to end.
The most perfect mother, teacher and best friend.

Taken

My grandchildren are very special to me.
There is one of them I do not see.
I tried to convince the mother to let me see her.
It was a definite no, because of some foolish misunderstanding
with the father.
I prayed every day to the heavenly Father,
That he will touch the heart of the mother,
And let her allow me to see my granddaughter.
The last time I saw her she was about eighteen months old.
She is now seven and oh, how she must have grown.
She is like a lamb that has been taken away.
I know I will see her again someday.
In Jesus's name I pray.

The Gift

My precious innocent baby is God's greatest gift to me
And, I love her unconditionally.
As I counted her fingers and toes
I wondered what our future together holds.

When I looked into her beautiful eyes
My heart was filled with joy and pride.
She is the only child I have got
And I thanked God for that.

Unfortunately, a few years later
Her mother took me out of the picture.
Because of some foolish misunderstanding
Our wonderful future was ruined.

I did put up a good fight
But mothers always get the rights.
Luckily I got to see her again when she was about five
And I missed not having her in my life.

Although we are apart
She will always be in my heart.
I prayed that one day I will see
My precious angel coming towards me,
Looking as beautiful as she could be.
Despite the fact I know not where she is,
She is and will forever be my most precious gift.

Put God First

Your illness is not a curse
Nevertheless, it could get better or even worse.
God is not punishing you.
He only allows the devil control, to see what you would do.
Have faith in God and trust Him,
In prayer, praise and worshiping.
Do not pray just because you want to get better.
Put God first in your life
And everything else will come after.

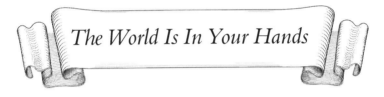

The World Is In Your Hands

Dear God, the world is in Your hands.
Help us to understand and appreciate
The things you have done
And are doing and will do in our lives each day.
Dear Lord, help us not to stray when things do not go our way.
Give us the strength and courage to look up to You and pray,
For the world is in Your hands.
You are Lord, and God of all, ruler of the universe,
The one and true living God
And the world is in Your hands.
Let us count our blessings and not what is missing.
You are the provider and the world is in your hands.

The King Has Fallen

The king of the castle's wife
Went through a lot of hassles in her life.
She was determined to keep her marriage together,
While he went about with another.

Miles he would travel into town
To do whatever he wanted regardless of her frown.
Many times she would ask him to stay
But he ignored her and went on his way.

She waited and anticipated.
Once again was disappointed.
Suddenly he was stricken, an illness he couldn't seem to get over
And, his life became a disaster.

Trips to town he no longer takes
For the journey he is unable to make.
Memories of the past fill his heart with so much pain
He sometimes seems like he is going insane.

The king has fallen off his throne.
All he would do is whine and moan.
He needs to stop the mourning and complaining,
Thank God his is among the living,
And that his wife has stayed with him.

Dear Lord

Dear Lord, I have been having a lot of pain every day,
And it does not seem as if it intends to go away.
I have been taking medications, and they do not seem to be
   working.
I do not know what else to do, I now turn to you.
What I did last I should have done first.
Lord, forgive me as I look to you for mercy and grace.
Dear God forgive my sin and come into my heart today.
Give me the strength to do what I have to do,
And the courage to face whatever life throws my way.
Help me to think positive that all my fears and negative thoughts
   will fade away.
I will continue to praise and worship you every day.

My Little Miracle

When I was pregnant with my first child,
A baby girl was what I had in mind.
But God did not grant me my wish.
I had to take what was put into my dish.
Many years later, I still did not have my daughter.
However, I continued to give praise and thanks to my heavenly
    Father.
He has blessed me with my sons,
The miracles no one else could have done.
The devil was against me getting my daughter,
So he decided to enter the picture.
Unfortunately, I was diagnosed with cancer.
I never thought that this could happen to me.
Maybe my dream was not meant to be.
Then God shone some light on the picture
And miraculously, I received my answer.
My God and heavenly Father
Had blessed me with a beautiful daughter.
Again, the devil was mad about what God had done,
And he tried to take two of my sons.
And he still has not won.
As you all can see, my children are here with me.
And I thank God for His love, guidance, protection and mercy.

My Angel

As I look around I can see, the blessings God restored for me.
I feel so proud to be at my daughter's first graduation ceremony.
I will make sure she takes advantage of every opportunity
To become the woman God has created her to be.
As she promotes to another class,
I will help to prepare her for the difficult tasks,
So that every exam she will pass.
My daughter will soon be five,
Oh what joy she has brought to my life.
She has now started her educational journey.
In the future I hope to see that she graduates with honours from
    university.
When she is ready to face the world on her own,
Lord, please let her know that she is not alone.
She is the evidence of my faith, and the miracle God has created.
As my angel stood before me, with wings I cannot see,
I pray to God Almighty, that she will be strong and healthy.
And will live to see the age of at least sixty.
Lord, may I push it a little further to seventy.
I also pray that she will embrace your love, blessings and mercy.
Thank you for hearing me,
I will now be still and wait on thee.

Without You

Jesus I love you; Jesus I praise you.
Without you I am nothing, without you I cannot do anything.
You are my eyes, without you I am blind.
You are my ears, without you I am deaf.
You are my mouth, without you I am speechless.
Jesus I love you, Jesus I praise you.
Without you I am nothing, without you I cannot do anything.
You are my hands, without you they are useless.
You are my feet, without you they are motionless.
You are my life, without you I am dead.
Jesus I love you, Jesus I praise you.
Without you I am nothing, without you I cannot do anything.

Never Forget

When trials and temptations come your way
Never do you forget to pray.
When your back is pushed against the wall
Be courageous and stand tall.
Never forget God's mercy and grace.
Never forget to seek His face.
Never forget to give Him praise.
Never forget where God has brought you from.
Look forward to where He is taking you,
To higher heights and deeper depths
Where your life will be blessed
Hallelujah!

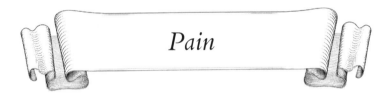

Pain

Pain is something our brain tells us is there.
If we wrapped ourselves in prayer,
The Holy Spirit will appear,
Then we will realise the pain is not really there.

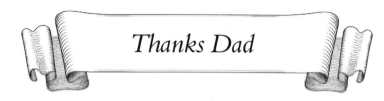

Thanks Dad

On this special day created by God, indicated by man,
I pray to the almighty thanking him for the male role model in my
    life,
Who has always been able to show positivity, regardless of the
    situation.
He made sure I ate even if he had to stay hungry.
Expecting the best from me but satisfied with the minimum that I
    achieved.
He taught me how to deal with difficult times,
And appreciate the good ones.
He told me to be there for my siblings regardless of the
    consequence,
And showed me love without saying.
As human we will always want more than we have
But must learn to accept and appreciate what we do have.

A True Friend

The thought of thoughts and dream of dreams,
Things we all have been through.
Headache and pain we suffered the same,
And the wishes that did not come true.
We cry and wail when relationships fail
Thinking the world has come to an end.
A hug will appear, tissues to wipe your tears
And the whispering voice of a true friend.

Déjà Vu

I dreamt a dream like déjà vu, of beauty most divine.
I felt so secure, a drug I need all the time.
The childlike angel bow at the ready,
The coordinates locked, and aligned.
A bull's eye shot, the target I got,
And now, you are my valentine.

A Dream

I dreamt a dream of insanity
That you could be in love with me.
I felt a feel of magical touch,
As you walked by, our hands brushed.
My heart skipped a beat, my hairs stood up.
I thought, 'Ooh, goose bumps, what a rush'.

As I open my eyes and look to the sky,
I thank the Lord, no question why.
This beautiful creature his angel from above
The one with whom I have fallen in love.
Hear me oh Lord as I kneel, I pray
I will marry this precious angel someday.
Let us love, care and cherish each other forever
As we praise and worship together.

Hold My Hand

Dear Lord you said the years of our days are three scores and ten.
I am only half a score.
It means that there are twenty, plus twenty, plus twenty more.
Lord you also said that if by reason of strength it can go to eighty.
Wow! That sounds plenty.
Lord I pray that those years will be given to me.
I know it is a lot I am asking of thee.
You are our Father in heaven
And you said ask, and it shall be given.
Lord, hold my hand and lead the way
As I follow thee, step by step every day.
And Lord, bless my family.
Especially my mummy and daddy.
In Jesus's name I pray.

Some Day

I want to go to heaven someday.
Sit beside my Jesus and hear him say:
'Well done my good and faithful servant, come and stay.
You have made it to heaven.
You have made it all the way.'

Blessings

Every day you watch and pray for guidance and protection,
Strength and perseverance, through life's trials and tribulations
And, for granting of blessing from your Father above,
Who heard and blessed you with His precious love.
He gave you children and your grandchildren you have lived to
    see.
Soon you will have your great-grandchildren listening to your
    stories and receiving your love.
So much is your blessing, as the blessing of Israel,
The gift gave to you, from your Father above.

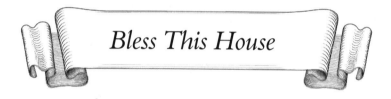

Bless This House

Dear God, bless this house and all who dwell within.
Bless those who visited just to say hello
And who came and stayed for a week or so.
I pray that they accept You into their hearts
Live a righteous life, walk the straight and narrow path.
Bless them spiritually, physically and financially.
I pray that they will praise and worship you daily.

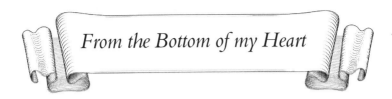

From the Bottom of my Heart

Thank you God for the rain that is falling,
Thank you for the sun that is shining,
Thank you for the wind that is blowing,
Thank you for the air I am inhaling.
Thank you for guiding my path,
Thank you from the bottom of my heart.

Teach Your Children

Take a look around the village you live in.
Is there fighting, shooting or killing?
Think about the things you can do or say
That will help keep the sorrow and pain away.
When your children get into a fight
Do not tell them to walk with a knife.
Teach them the facts of life.
Neither should you tell them to walk with a gun.
Teach them how to pray and walk with Jesus, God's son.
That is the most powerful weapon.

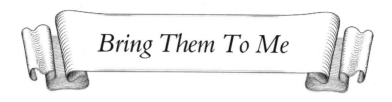

Bring Them To Me

Do not carry your sins everywhere with you.
Bring them to me I will take them from you.
Jesus, may I give you my sickness and diseases too?
Of course, I will take them all from you.
Thank you Jesus, I feel as light as a feather.
Thank you for replacing my storm with such beautiful weather.
If I had wings I would fly
And soar like an eagle in the sky.

Bless This Kitchen

Dear Lord, bless this little kitchen
And the food that is prepared within.
Bless those who entered occasionally
To have a cup of tea, or coffee.
Bless the pots, plates, knives and forks.
Bless those who sat down to eat and talk.

On This Special Day

On this special day I celebrate another year of life and love
That is given to me by my Father above.
The day I invited him into my heart
He promised to protect and guide my path.
He gave me the chance to become a wife and mother
And I will continue to serve him and not another.
Lord you have blessed me so richly
My third generation I have lived to see.
I am now at the age of seventy.
You said if by reason of strength it can go to eighty.
Lord I pray that those years are in store for me.
Each one, that added to my number
I will surely welcome them without murmur.

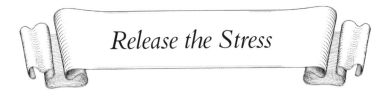

Release the Stress

Whenever you go to the bathroom to do
What someone else cannot do for you,
And there is no one to disturb you,
These are some things you can do:
You can meditate on the word of God,
And sing the glorious song that comes into your heart.
It will help to release the stress
And your life will be blessed.

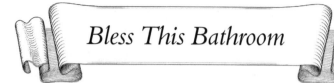

Bless This Bathroom

Lord bless this bathroom,
And all those who would enter
to do one thing or another.
It is the quietest place in the house
Where I can give you all my attention
During meditation and without any interruption.

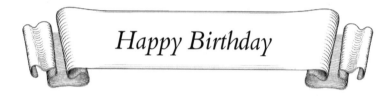

Happy Birthday

Another year you have lived to see, thanks to grace, persistence and
  prayer.
His loyal soldier you have proved to be, each and every year.
Love and guidance He will give to you whilst travelling your
  chosen path.
For his home you have prepared for him deep within your heart.

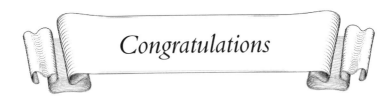

You are going to have the baby you anxiously wanted.
Patiently, you have waited.
May your wish be granted.
I pray that your baby will be a boy
And fill your heart with pride and joy.

Give Thanks

Thank you God for my life and your love,
Thank you for the blessings from above.
Thank you for the roof over my head,
Thank you for getting me out of bed.
Thank you for being so good to me,
Thank you for my family.

Thank you God for the food I eat,
Thank you for the shoes on my feet.
Thank you for the clothes I wear,
Thank you for being there.

Thank you God for the years you have given to me,
I am looking forward to the age of seventy.
If there are more in store for me,
I will welcome them gracefully.

Thank you for being my best friend,
I promise to stay close to you until the very end.
Thank you for being there when I needed you most,
Thanks to the Father, Son and Holy Ghost.

Thank God

Thank you God for another year of life and love
That is filled with blessings, from above.
Thank you for giving me thy great salvation so rich and free.
Lord you said the years of our days are seventy.
And, if by reason of strength it can go to eighty.
Lord I have already past the age of eighty.
With your blessing and favour, I pray that I reach ninety,
And will see the fourth generation of my family.

Lord cast me not off in time of old age
Although I feel like I am trapped in a cage.
For long life thou had given me
So forsake me not when my strength failed me.
Lord you are the light and lifter up of my soul
Take your place in my life and make me whole.
Lord you are my best friend,
And, I will walk with you to the very end.
Lord if there is anything I fail of asking thee,
Fail not Lord, to grant it unto me.

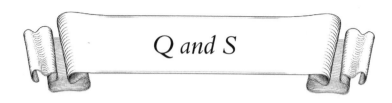

Q and S

Do you despise any of your children's partners?
Do you not see them or your grandchildren because of the
    animosity?
Do you ever think of them as a blessing from God Almighty?
Do you ever think about the people who would like to have
    children but cannot?
Do you ever think about the people who would like to have even
    one grandchild and have none?
Do you ever think about how to avoid the animosity?
Do you ever try to leave it in the past where it belongs?
Do you ever try walking while looking back?
Do you ever notice you cannot see where you are going?
Do you ever think about forgiving that person for whatever they
    have done?
Do you ever think about forgiving yourself for holding on so long?
Do you ever think about asking God to forgive you?
No matter what you do or say,
You cannot bring yesterday to today.
Let go of the anger and pain.
You have much more to gain.
You held that animosity for so long,
Yet God still blesses you with life.
And he probably gave you a husband or a wife.

The Miracle

He overdosed himself with his medications and went to bed.
Then told his partner that when she wakes in the morning he will
    be dead.
'God would not do me such injustice,' she said.
'He would not let you die beside me in bed.'
Not knowing what he had done,
She decided to put the matter into God's hand.
She woke up a few times to have a wee
And saw him sleeping peacefully.
As she laid silently on the bed,
His words echoed repeatedly in her head
But she drove them out with prayers instead
And refused to believe that she would wake up and find him dead.
When she woke up in the morning and did not see him,
She was terrified and went towards the kitchen,
And there he was at the table eating.
She whispered a prayer and took a seat
As her heart returned to its regular beat.
He sometimes saw things that were not there
And heard things that she could not hear.
In the evening when he confessed to her what he had done,
Angry and frustrated she took him to the hospital.
They then told her that the critical period had already past,
And she thanked God from deep within her heart.
Whenever you are going through a storm,
Just call on Jesus; a miracle he will perform.
If God is not ready to take you,
Whatever you try to do he will not let harm befall you.